Someday HEAVEN

There are some things the Lord our God has kept secret.
But there are some things he has let us know.
These things belong to us and our children forever.

DEUTERONOMY 29:29

For my family,
Laura, Matthew & Melissa

If I get to Heaven first,
I'll scout out the best hiking trails.
I love you.

Someday HEAVEN

By Larry Libby · Illustrations by Tim Jonke

Gold 'n' Honey BOOKS

SOMEDAY HEAVEN
Published by Gold'n'Honey Books
a part of the Questar publishing family
© 1993 Questar Publishers, Inc.

International Standard Book Number: 0-945564-77-5

Printed in Italy

For information:
QUESTAR PUBLISHERS, INC.
POST OFFICE BOX 1720
SISTERS, OREGON 97759

Someday...Heaven

Have you ever wondered about God's home?

Have you ever sat on a grassy hill on a summer afternoon and looked as far
as you could look into the deep blue?
Where does God live? Where is God when He's at home?
What a home it must be!

Have you ever watched the clouds when the sun slips low in the sky?
A cooling breeze stirs the grass and whispers in the leaves.
The blue of the sky washes away into crimson and pink and purple.
The grand billowy clouds ride high and proud into the coming night and sometimes...
sometimes before you see the first little star...

you can almost see castles and great houses in the clouds...

you can almost imagine the setting sun reflecting gold and red off Heaven's high windows.

Does God's home look like that? Does He like living there?
Is He ever lonesome?
Does He like having company?
Will He take me to His home someday...after I die?
What will it be like?

We have so many questions about Heaven, God's Forever Home.

The Bible tells us just a little, and we need to understand what it says.
But I don't think God would mind if we used our imaginations a little, too.

Do you?

WHERE IS HEAVEN?

The Bible says that Heaven is *up*. When God looks at Earth from Heaven, He looks *down*. The book of Psalms says, *The Lord looks down from Heaven. He sees every person. From his throne he watches everyone who lives on earth (Psalm 33:13-14).*

One night long ago God sent a dream to a man named Jacob. In that dream, Jacob saw a stairway reaching *up* into the night sky. Can you close your eyes and see those steps shining white in the moonlight—climbing and climbing into a field of stars? The stairs went all the way into Heaven. Jacob watched as the angels of God walked *down* the stairs to Earth and *up* the stairs to Heaven.

When Jesus left Earth to go back to Heaven, He went *up* until He disappeared into a cloud! But He didn't need a stairway. He just lifted His hands and *up* He went. The people who were with Jesus scrunched up their eyes and stared into the sky. They watched as He rose higher and higher in the air—like a balloon that floats so high in the wind it looks like a tiny silver pin stuck into the wide blue.

While the people were staring and squinting and pointing, two angels appeared beside them. Everyone must have jumped half a foot in the air when the angels suddenly spoke. (Angels may not mean to startle people, but it seems as if they always do.)

"Why are you looking *up*?" asked the angels. "Don't you know that Jesus will come back again?"

Some wonderful day, Jesus will come back for us. He will come *down* from Heaven with a shout! And the Bible says we will be "gathered *up*" into the clouds to meet the Lord in the air! If we're still on Earth when that happens, we won't need a stairway, either. As quick as your eye can blink, as quick as your heart can beat, we'll fly high into the sky and meet the Lord Jesus in the air. I think you'll get the biggest hug of your life on the fluffy top of a big white cloud!

Yes, Heaven is a real place, and it is *up*. But where? Is Heaven a perfect planet, far away in a distant galaxy? Is Heaven tucked away in some secret corner of space?

The Bible doesn't say. But Jesus did tell us one thing. He is the only way to get there!

HOW DO I GET TO HEAVEN?

One day the Lord Jesus began telling His friends, "It's time for me to leave this world and go to My Father." He was saying good-bye! His friends felt so sad and upset they didn't know what to do. Their Lord and best Friend was *leaving* them. Going away. And He wasn't just leaving for another city or another country, He was going to leave *the Earth!*

Because His friends were so very worried and troubled, Jesus told them just a little bit about where He was going. (Sometimes I wish He had said more!) This is what He said:

Don't let your hearts be troubled. Trust in God. And trust in me. There are many rooms in my Father's house. I would not tell you this if it were not so. I am going there to prepare a place for you. After I go and prepare a place for you, I will

The Lord looks down from Heaven. He sees every person. From his throne he watches everyone who lives on earth.

PSALM 33:13-14

3

come back. Then I will take you to be with me so that you may be where I am (John 14:1-3).

Can you imagine Him looking around the room at the sad faces of those men? Everyone was probably hanging his head and scuffing his sandals and looking at the floor. They all probably had big lumps in their throats and tears hiding in the corners of their eyes.

Then Jesus said something that surprised them very much. He said, "You *know* the way to the place where I am going!"

Jesus' friends must have looked at each other, but no one said anything. No one, that is, until a man named Thomas blurted out just exactly what everyone was thinking. Thomas was a very honest man. He always said what was on his mind. Maybe the other men *wanted* to ask Jesus this question, but they were afraid or ashamed. Not Thomas! He spoke right up.

"Lord, we *don't* know where You are going. So *how* can we know the way?"

Maybe Thomas wanted Jesus to roll out a big map. Maybe he wanted Jesus to get out some colored pencils and a ruler and draw a big picture. Maybe he wanted Jesus to say, "Okay, Tom, this blue circle is Earth. This yellow ball is the sun. And way over here in this corner is this shimmery silvery star where I am going. And this is how I will get there."

But Jesus didn't open up a map. He didn't draw a picture. He didn't show a maze with a "Start Here" sign and "Finish Here" sign and all sorts of traps and dead-ends in between. He just looked Thomas right in the eyes and told him one thing.

I am the way. And I am the truth and the life. The only way to the Father is through me (John 14:6).

That's the only thing Thomas needed to know. And this is the most important thing *we* could ever learn about going to Heaven.

Have you ever heard your parents give directions to someone about how to get to your house? Perhaps they will say, "Just go down this road and turn right at the first stoplight. Then turn left at the big store, and go four blocks. Then look for the third house on the left with this number on the mailbox."

But the way to Heaven isn't a road.
It isn't a path.
It isn't a street.
It's a PERSON.

Jesus is the stairway to Heaven. Jesus is the door. Jesus is the road. Jesus is the only way anyone *ever* finds Heaven.

This is hard to understand, even for grownups. But it reminds me of a little boy I know—a boy with a very strong big brother. One day the little boy looked way up in a tree and saw his big brother sitting on a limb.

"I wish I could climb up there," the boy said.

"Come on up," said his brother.

"I can't," said the boy. "My arms aren't strong enough. I can't reach high enough. I could *never* get up that tree."

"Yes, you could!" said his big brother. And do you know what happened? The big brother slid down the tree, put his little brother on his back, and shinnied back up the tree to that big limb. He was so strong!

*I am the way.
And I am the
truth and the life.
The only way to
the Father is
through me.*
JOHN 14:6

5

"Now," said the big brother, "you can be with me where I am." And they sat together up on that fine, high limb, just as happy as a couple of birds.

That's just what Jesus has done for us. We could *never* climb up to where He lives. We could *never* be good enough to get up into God's Heaven on our own. We could *never* open Heaven's door by our own hard work.

But God wants us there! Jesus wants us there! That's why Jesus came all the way down from Heaven to show us the way. Only *He* is strong enough and good enough to open Heaven's door and take us inside.

WHO LIVES IN HEAVEN?

Have you ever picked up a phone book? You know the book I'm talking about…the big floppy one with the white pages and yellow pages and all those tiny names.

If you've ever been to a really big city, like Los Angeles or Chicago, you may have seen that their phone book is huge. It's so big that people stand on it to reach stuff in the top of the cupboard, or prop open the door with it, or put it on a dining room chair for a little kid to sit on so he can reach the table.

If you live in a little town like Sisters, Oregon, the phone book may be skinny. Standing on it wouldn't help you reach anything. It wouldn't hold open the door to a hamster cage. And if a little kid sat on 50 of them, he still couldn't reach the table.

What if Heaven had a phone book? How big would it be? And whose names would be in the book?

If you looked underneath the letter "G," I guess you'd find the name "God the Father." He wouldn't need a telephone of course, but He does like people to call Him. That's what He told Jeremiah.

CALL TO ME, AND I WILL ANSWER YOU, and show you great and mighty things, which you do not know (Jeremiah 33:3, NKJV).

You could look under "J" and find "Jesus." He has always lived in Heaven. But He was away for a time. The mighty Son of God left His bright home, and how Heaven must have missed Him! One cold starlit night many years ago He was born to a Jewish girl named Mary…in a stable…in a manger…in a little town called Bethlehem. That night was so wonderful and amazing that the angels still talk about it. I think they always will.

You could look under "H" and find the "Holy Spirit." He is the same Friend and Helper who lives inside everyone who loves Jesus. He is in Heaven, too. Jesus said the Holy Spirit will be with us forever.

You would see lots and lots of angels' names. They've lived in Heaven for a long, long time, so they must really know their way around. We don't know many of their names now—only Michael and Gabriel—but someday we will know them all. Maybe we'll call them up and talk to them. Wouldn't that be fun?

"Hello, Gabriel? This is Heather. There's a purple-and-green planet over in the next galaxy I'd love to see. How about packing a lunch and exploring it with me?"(I wonder what an angel would bring for lunch. Something good, I'll bet.)

6

Peter and James and John and Philip and all the rest.

Oh, and then so many other names. Names of brave men and women who gave up their homes and even their lives for Jesus. Names of parents and children who loved God and obeyed His Word even when the whole world hated them and turned against them. Names of people from China and Egypt and Ireland and India and Russia and countries that don't even exist any more! The names of your own mother's mother's mother and father's father's father might be there.

And of course there will be so many babies who died before they ever had a chance to live. They may not have even had names here on Earth. But they do in Heaven. God knows their names. And how God loves those babies! Maybe when we get to Heaven they will be grown-up people full of laughter and life and love for God. How good it will be to talk to them and be with them.

Jesus said that whoever believes in Him will have his name or her name written down in a book in Heaven. It isn't a phone book. It's called the Book of Life, and it is very big. Inside that book are the names of all the people who will be in Heaven.

Are you very sure that your name is in that Book? You can be! Just take a peek at the last chapter in this book.

You would see the names of millions of people who lived before Jesus came to Earth. They trusted in God, too, and looked forward to the day when He would send a Savior. You could start with "A" and find "Abel" or "Adam" or jump over to "Z" and get a number for "Zedekiah" or "Zephaniah."

The names of Jesus' twelve special followers would be there:

WHAT IS THE CLOSEST I CAN BE TO HEAVEN?

Some people feel closest to Heaven when they are up in the mountains. Way up on the snowy roof of our world, looking down at the distant towns and valleys…they feel a little bit nearer to their Forever Home.

Some people feel closest to Heaven when they are out on a ship at sea. Out, out in the rolling blue ocean, long miles away from the troubles of the land…they feel a deep peace in their hearts and maybe just a tiny bit closer to the wide, peaceful land of Heaven.

Some people feel closest to Heaven as they are walking in a field at twilight. Just listening to the crickets and the wind rustling the grass, smelling the cool fragrance of faraway trees and dew-drenched hillsides and sweet, sun-ripened hay, they feel nudged up just a little closer to Heaven's door.

Have you ever walked and talked just to Jesus?

Have you ever sat alone in a quiet place and whispered secret things to your Heavenly Father? Have you ever heard Him whisper quiet words back into your heart?

Those times help us feel closer to Heaven, I think.

Have you ever sung songs of praise to Jesus with people who love Him with all their hearts? Have you ever seen the light of joy on their faces and tears of joy in their eyes? Have you felt your heart almost burst with happiness as the sweet music fills a room and spills out the windows?

In those times, I think Heaven comes very near.

Or just maybe Heaven was near all along… and we didn't even know it!

HOW LONG DOES IT TAKE TO GET TO HEAVEN?

It may not take any longer than closing your eyes on Earth—and opening them up in Heaven! But we know one thing for sure…it won't take longer than one day to get there!

When the Lord Jesus was put on a cross to die, two other men were put on crosses, too. One was on one side of Jesus, and one was on the other side. Both men had done bad things. They were being killed in this terrible way as a punishment.

The man on one of the crosses began yelling at Jesus, calling Him names and making fun of Him. But the man on the other side of Jesus told him to be quiet! He said:

You should fear God! You are getting the same punishment as he is. We are punished justly; we should die. But this man has done nothing wrong! (Luke 23:40-41).

Then he turned his head toward Jesus and looked into His eyes. And even though both men were hurting so much, they spoke to each other.

"Jesus!" the man said in a choked voice. "Jesus! Remember me when…when You come into Your kingdom!"

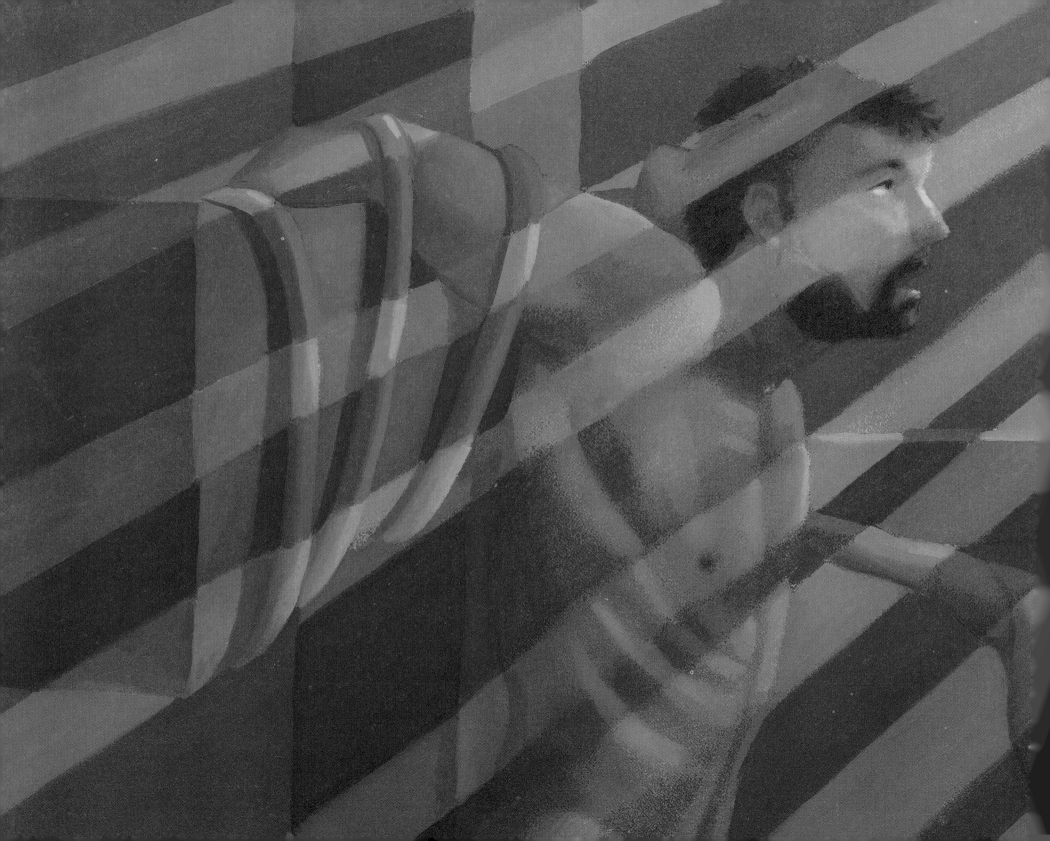

Then Jesus said to him, *"Listen! What I say is true: Today you will be with me in paradise!" (Luke 23:43).*

Within a few hours, Jesus and both of the other men died. And on that very day, Jesus and the man who had prayed to Him on the cross were both in Heaven!

Jesus had kept His promise. "You'll be in Heaven with Me," He had said, "and we'll be there TODAY!"

Many years later the apostle Paul wrote his friends in the city of Corinth. Paul seemed to say that as soon as we die, we will be with the Lord Jesus. Here is what he wrote:

So we always have courage. We know that while we live in this body, we are away from the Lord…And we really want to be away from this body and at home with the Lord (2 Corinthians 5:6,8).

So how long does it take to get to Heaven? Well, for sure it doesn't take any longer than one day. And Paul seems to say that you are either at home in your body on Earth, or you are away from your body and at home in Heaven!

One good man I know explained it this way. Did you ever fall asleep in the living room watching TV, eating cookies, and drinking milk, and then wake up in the morning in your warm bed? How do you think that happened? Well, let me tell you. When you fell asleep, someone who loves you very much, came and picked you up and carried you gently into your bedroom. Without even waking you up, your mother or father put your pajamas on you, tucked you in bed, pulled the covers around you, and left you to sleep all night long.

That's exactly what the Lord does for us when we die. We fall asleep down here on Earth and wake up in God's house!

"Today you will be with me in paradise!"
LUKE 23:43

11

WILL MY PETS GO TO HEAVEN?

Our wise Creator must have had such a good time creating animals. God knew just what He was doing when He made kittens soft and playful. And hamsters shy and whiskery. And horses strong and proud. And can't you imagine Him smiling when He designed the face of a dog? It was God who gave dogs their cold noses, soft droopy ears, funny faces, and floppy tongues.

When God had created all the animals in the world, He said, "It is GOOD!"

But since death followed sin into the world way back at the beginning, all the animals and people in the world have to die. The Bible says people live forever after they die, either in Heaven or away from Heaven. But the Bible doesn't say if animals live forever. If they do, God has decided not to tell us so.

God has given people a lot of love in their hearts. And He has given us many things to love. Some things we will love for just a short time. Some things we will love forever. Our wonderful pets may be friends we love for just a little while and then say good-bye to.

I'm glad that in Heaven there are *no more good-byes*. Everything we love in Heaven will be there always. And I wouldn't be surprised if there were...

the strangest
and funniest
and cuddliest
and friendliest
and grandest

animals in Heaven that you have ever seen! Our God loves surprises. And who knows? Maybe He will surprise us with a pet we loved very much on Earth.

Our God can do anything!

HOW LONG WILL I BE IN HEAVEN?

When you are in the car on a long, boring ride, time seems to go on and on. You begin to think you'll never get there. It seems as if the clock has slo-o-o-o-owed down like a sleepy snail crossing a sidewalk.

But when you're at your best friend's house, laughing and playing a really good game, time goes by so fast you can hardly believe it. Your mom says be home in one hour, and time goes ZIP! WHIZZ! The hands seem to fly around the clock. You just get started on your game and it's already time to go home!

Time goes slow when we are bored, or tired, or sad, or lonely. Time goes fast when we are excited, having fun, doing new

things, laughing, and enjoying people we love.

Oh…and just when the good times really get going, it's time to quit. It's time to get your coat and leave. It's time to climb out of the pool. It's time to drop out of the swing. It's time to get off your bike. It's time to say good-bye.

Our life here on Earth is full of quitting and leaving and moving and putting away and letting go and saying good-byes. Maybe you can remember saying in your heart, Oh this day is so good—I wish it could last forever!

That's what Heaven is. It's a good day that lasts forever.

The golden light will never fade into dark. The little flowers in the meadow will never die or wither. The fresh, excited feeling you have when you bound out of bed in the morning will never wear off. The joy will never turn into disappointment. The fun will never change into something you feel sorry about. The laughter and happiness will never be spoiled by having to leave or quit or say good-bye.

Really, time won't go fast or slow, because there will be no time at all! If you stopped an angel and said, "Please sir, what time is it?" He would just laugh and say, "Why, it's right now and it's forever!"

It will never be time to leave our friends. It will never be time to walk off into the dark. It will never be time to feel a lump in your throat because someone you love is going away. Daddies will never pack suitcases and get on airplanes. Mommies will never kiss you good-bye and leave you with someone else. Friends will never move away. Grandfathers and grandmothers will never get sick and die.

Jesus will see to all that. And even though Jesus may be the busiest person in all of Heaven, He will never be too busy to laugh with you or sail a boat with you or fly a kite with you or go for a walk with you for about a million years or so. Do you know what He said?

I will never leave you; I will never forget you. And, *You can be sure that I will be with you always (Hebrews 13:5; Matthew 28:20).*

I like that word ALWAYS, don't you?

And when our Lord Jesus makes a promise, nothing in the wide world or the wider Heavens can ever break it.

You can be sure that I will be with you always.
MATTHEW 28:20

13

WHAT IF I GET
TIRED OF BEING IN HEAVEN?

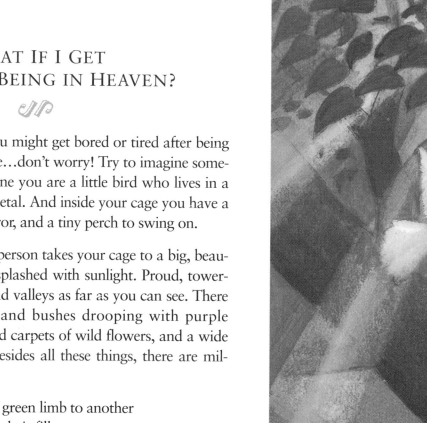

*So you
will go out with
joy. You will be led
out in peace.
The mountains
and the hills will
burst out in song
before you.
All the trees of the
fields will clap
their hands.*

ISAIAH 55:12

If you are thinking you might get bored or tired after being in Heaven for a while…don't worry! Try to imagine something with me. Imagine you are a little bird who lives in a tiny cage made of rusty metal. And inside your cage you have a food dish, and a little mirror, and a tiny perch to swing on.

Then one day some kind person takes your cage to a big, beautiful forest. The forest is splashed with sunlight. Proud, towering trees cover the hills and valleys as far as you can see. There are gushing waterfalls, and bushes drooping with purple berries, and fruit trees, and carpets of wild flowers, and a wide blue sky to fly in. And besides all these things, there are millions of other little birds…

> hopping from one green limb to another
> and eating their fill
> and raising their little families
> and singing their hearts out
> all through the day.

Now, little bird, can you imagine wanting to stay in your cage? Can you imagine saying, "Oh please don't let me go. I will miss my cage. I will miss my little food dish with seeds in it. I will miss my plastic mirror and my tiny little perch. I might get bored in that big forest."

That would be silly, wouldn't it? And it's just as silly to think we might run out of things to do in Heaven!

14

If you like to sing and praise the Lord now, you'll love it even more in Heaven. Our future Home will be filled with songs and music so beautiful and good it will bring tears of joy to your eyes.

Listen to the way Isaiah talks about that future day:

> *So you will go out with joy.*
> *You will be led out in peace.*
> *The mountains and the hills will burst out*
> *in song before you.*
> *All the trees of the fields will clap their hands*
> *(Isaiah 55:12).*

That's right! Someday you may be walking through Heaven, singing a little song to the Lord, and suddenly...

the great snowy mountains will begin singing with you in deep down voices that shake the ground...

the rolling, light-dappled hills will join in the chorus...

the trees of the forest will sway to the music and clap their branches...

the stream running through the field will laugh out loud and add her harmony...

even the rocks will sing along in their rumbly-tumbly voices.

If you like to make things with your hands now...think what it will be like to have all the time you could ever want to dream, and shape, and build, and dip your paintbrush in a thousand rainbows. The wise Creator of all things will be there to teach you!

Even though the Bible doesn't tell us much about what we will do, we know there will be a never-ending universe to run. I think God will allow us to help Him in all that He does. There may be cities to build and clouds to paint and worlds to watch and stars to tend and projects so high and huge and amazing that we can't even picture them in our minds.

There will always be new things to see, new places to go, new friends to laugh and run with. If you explored a new planet with a new friend every day you wouldn't run out of planets or friends in a million million years.

The Bible talks about resting in Heaven, but don't let that worry you. I don't think it will be the kind of resting where you have to go to bed or take a nap and miss all the fun.

I think it will be the kind of resting you do on a warm summer day...when you lie on your back on a green hillside and chew on a long piece of grass and listen to the whisper of the wind.

I think it will be the kind of resting you do at the seashore... when you bury your toes in the warm sand and listen to the sea gulls and watch the great green-blue waves rolling and rolling in.

Finding things to do will be no problem at all. Between worshiping and working and resting and exploring, the problem may be knowing what to do next.

But the first and best thing will always be praising our good God for taking us to His Forever Home.

IF HEAVEN IS SO GOOD, WHY ARE PEOPLE AFRAID TO DIE?

Why are we afraid of anything? We're afraid of things we don't understand. We're afraid of things we can't see. We're afraid of things that might hurt us.

We're afraid of the door called "death" because we've never been through that door before. We don't know what it will be like. We don't know if it will hurt. We don't want to go through it alone. We don't want to leave loved ones behind.

Even Christians who love the Lord Jesus and KNOW FOR SURE that Heaven is on the other side of the door may still be afraid to die. The Bible says that death is an enemy. It is the last enemy we will ever have to face.

Christ must rule until God puts all enemies under Christ's control. The last enemy to be destroyed is death (1 Corinthians 15:25-26).

Death was not what God wanted for His people. But when Adam and Eve chose to sin and disobey God, death came into the world right behind sin! Now it will be here until the Lord Jesus takes it away forever. And someday, He will!

But for now, death means saying good-bye to this world and going to a new world. It makes us sad to say good-bye to friends and family. That's the sad part of this world—there are so many good-byes.

But Heaven is full of hellos! We will say hello to old friends and new friends. We will say hello to Moses and Jonah and Peter and King David and Zacchaeus and Mary, the mother of Jesus, and billions of angels and millions of other people who love God. Every day will be full of happy hellos. There won't be any more good byes, only see-you-laters, because we will never run out of time to be with those we love.

And even though we may be afraid and sad to go through death's door, we won't really be alone. David knew Jesus would be with him. David said, *Even though I walk through the valley of the shadow of death, I will fear no evil, for you are with me (Psalm 23:4, NIV).* Jesus is always with us!

Have you ever met a new friend who said, "Come over to my house and play"? It will be the same way when it's time to go to Heaven. Jesus will say, "Come on into My Father's house! Come on inside!" And in you will go to the brightest and happiest place you have ever seen.

So you see…going to Heaven isn't just going *out* through death's door. It's coming *in* to the best place you could ever be.

Even though I walk through the valley of the shadow of death, I will fear no evil, for you are with me.

PSALM 23:4

17

WILL THERE BE
ROOM IN HEAVEN FOR ME?

Jesus told His friends, *There are many rooms in my Father's house. I would not tell you this if it were not true. After I go and prepare a place for you, I will come back* (John 14:2).

What do you imagine when you think about these words? Do you imagine one very, very large house with long, long hallways and tall towers and great winding stairways and millions and millions of rooms?

What a house that would be! Maybe Queen Esther's room would be down the hall, King David's room would be just upstairs, and your great-great-grandma would be next door! Maybe at suppertime an angel would ring a bell and everyone would come tumbling out of his room. All the people would slide down the long banisters and sit around a table that goes for a million miles in each direction. (That would be a very long way to pass the potatoes.)

It probably isn't like that at all.

For some reason, Jesus didn't tell us much about His Father's house. But He did say He was going to prepare a place for us...and that makes me wonder.

The Bible says Jesus created *everything* in just seven days. He created...
> every kind of bird,
>> every kind of fish,
>>> the deep blue oceans,
>>>> the tall, snow-topped mountains,

There are many rooms in my father's house. I would not tell you this if it were not true. After I go and prepare a place for you, I will come back.

JOHN 14:2

19

the vast green forests,
the rolling fields of golden grain,
the mighty rushing rivers,
every star that sparkles in the night...
AND—so many worlds and wonders and amazing places scattered across the wide, wide miles of space that we could never even get a tiny peek at all of them in a billion years.

He did all that in *seven days*. And He has been working and working and working on our new home in Heaven for...how long? Almost *two thousand years*. Oh, what ever could it be like?

What He wanted to tell His friends (including you and me) was that there is lots of room in His Father's house. We will explore it forever and never come to the end of it. And do you know what? He is preparing one special place in Heaven just for you.

A place? What kind of place? Is it a room? A house? A castle? A world? A star? That's part of His surprise! But whatever it is, it will be the right and best place, because Jesus is getting it ready just for you. And who knows what you like or what you need more than Jesus? He's taking His time making your special place, because He loves you more than I can say.

WILL MY GRANDPA STILL BE OLD IN HEAVEN?

Your Grandpa will have a brand new body in Heaven. His back won't hurt him when he gets up in the morning. He won't need glasses. He won't need a hearing aid. He won't need false teeth. He won't walk all humped over or lean on a cane. He won't have to stay away from spicy foods. He won't have to throw a baseball underhand because of a sore shoulder. He won't have trouble remembering things.

The Bible says that the bodies we have on Earth aren't the right kind to live forever. They just wear out—like your favorite sneakers or your brother's old bicycle. We need to trade them in for new ones. And how wonderful those new bodies will be! They won't get tired or need sleep. They won't get hurt or have aches and pains. They will be able to run and run and run and never grow tired.

You've never seen your Grandpa like that! Even your Grandma, who met him when he was young and full of energy, never saw him like that! He will be like Jesus. He will never get sick again. He won't have to take pills. He won't need operations. He won't rub smelly stuff on his hurting muscles. He won't ever feel bad or cranky or forget to keep his promises.

And if your Grandpa is already in Heaven, he will never, never have to grow old and die again.

How will you know what he looks like when you get there? Well, maybe he will still whistle the same tune, or have the same twinkle in his eye, or still like to go fishing. Maybe he'll still call you "Punkin," or "Rascal," or "Princess," or whatever he likes to call you now. Maybe he'll still give you a peppermint drop, a kiss on the cheek, or mess up your hair. Maybe he'll still wear "Old Spice" after shave lotion.

But you will know him and he will know you. And if you want to, I'll bet you can go fishing with him for about a thousand years after you get there.

22

WHO ARE THE ANGELS?

Angels are God's letter carriers. Well, yes, I'm sure they do more than that. The Bible says they are spirits who serve God and are sent to help those who love Jesus.

But time after time God has sent His angels through Heaven's door to carry important messages to Earth. How God loves the world! How much He wants to communicate with the people He created for Himself!

The Bible tells us how God has sent message after message to His people. He has sent important information. He has sent stern warnings. And most of all, He has sent love letters. But how did God's mail get through to people on Earth? Lots of times, by ANGEL EXPRESS.

Most people who have seen angels have been afraid of them. God's letter carriers are swift and powerful and beautiful and so white and shining you can hardly look at them. Fresh from the bright land of Heaven, angels arrive on Earth looking like a flash of lightning in a dark evening sky.

Usually the first thing angels have to tell people is, "Don't be afraid! Don't faint! Don't run away! I'm just an angel with an air mail message from God."

Some of the messages have been very sad. God has told His people the terrible things that would happen because they disobeyed Him. Some of the messages have made people cry and pray hard that God would forgive them and help them.

Other messages have told people what would happen in the far-away future.

But the job angels seem to like best (and probably all get in line for) is bringing good news to Earth. Do you remember hearing about the night long ago when Jesus was born? Beneath a star-sprinkled sky, the shepherds were quietly watching over their flocks of sleepy sheep. All at once—

An angel of the Lord stood before them. The glory of the Lord was shining around them, and suddenly they became very frightened. The angel said to them, "Don't be afraid, because I am bringing you some good news. Today your Savior was born in David's town. He is Christ the Lord" (Luke 2:9-10).

That angel had the happy job of bringing absolutely wonderful news. And then it was as if Heaven's door suddenly flew wide open and a million other angels said, "Oh, this is *too much* good news for one angel! We want to deliver the message, too! Let us say the good news, too!" And then all of God's letter carriers seemed to come tumbling out of Heaven in a great, excited rush—singing and shouting and praising God and chasing away the darkness of night.

Years and years later, another angel (or maybe it was the same lucky one) got to tell the best news of all.

When Jesus rose from the dead on the very first Easter, that angel put his strong shoulder against the big stone that covered the Lord's tomb. The angel rolled it back and then sat on it! (Do you suppose he sat very straight and stern...or sort of smiled and leaned back and crossed his legs?)

He said to two women who were looking for the Lord's dead body, *Why are you looking for a living person here? This is a place for the dead. Jesus is not here. He has risen from death! (Luke 24:5-6).*

Don't be afraid, because I am bringing you some good news. Today your Savior was born in David's town. He is Christ the Lord.

LUKE 2:9-10

23

Angels love to be God's letter carriers. They love being the Angel Express. And God's messages do get delivered, even when Satan wants to stop them.

But tell me, if God loves us so much, why does He use the Angel Express? Why doesn't God leave His beautiful home and deliver the messages to our poor old world Himself? Why doesn't He come to where we live and show us His strong, forever love? He DID, didn't He?

The best and brightest of all God's love letters came special delivery to Bethlehem. The Lord Jesus not only brought the message of love, He *was* the message of love. He was the best Gift God could have ever sent to Earth.

No wonder those angels got so excited!

WILL IT ALWAYS BE LIGHT IN HEAVEN?

I know a little boy who couldn't sleep unless his mom or dad left the hall light on. He didn't like the dark. But the soft light coming from the hall shone into his bedroom a little and helped him scrunch down into his covers and fall asleep. That boy would be glad to read about the light in Heaven. If you know him or someone like him, why don't you show him these words from the Bible:

(Heaven's) city does not need the sun or the moon to shine on it. The glory of God is its light, and the Lamb is the city's lamp (Revelation 21:23).

Our Forever Home won't need the sun and moon. It won't

need starlight or firelight or streetlights or flashlights or head-lights or nightlights. The Lord God will be all the light we will ever need.

Does that seem strange? It really isn't. The moon borrows its light from the sun, and the sun borrows its light from Jesus. All the light that ever existed is borrowed from Jesus.

Jesus said, "I am the light of the world. The person who follows me will never live in darkness. He will have the light that gives life" (John 8:12).

In Heaven, there will be no darkness to be afraid of, or stumble in. There will be no darkness to end our fun or cloud our eyes or cast the smallest shadow over our happiness.

> The Light will fill the air.
> The Light will fill our eyes.
> The Light will fill our hearts.
> The Light will never fade.

Now we have darkness. Now there are dark streets and dark rooms and dark corners and dark words and dark hearts. But even here in our sometimes-dark world we can have some of Heaven's light! The Bible says:

Your word is a lamp to my feet and a light for my path (Psalm 119:105).

Until we leave Earth's darkness behind to enjoy Heaven's always-light, the Bible can help us see the way we ought to go and the things we ought to do and the words we ought to say. It is like a bright and burning lamp that chases back the shadows and shows us where to walk.

Isn't God good to lend us some light until we get Home?

DO I HAVE TO DIE TO SEE HEAVEN?

Almost everybody who has seen Heaven has had to die first. But God has allowed some of His people to take a peek into Heaven while they were still alive on Earth. A man named Isaiah saw God sitting on a high throne in Heaven with angels all around Him. Another man named Micaiah saw the same thing—and a little bit more:

I saw the Lord sitting on his throne. His Heavenly army was standing near him on his right and on his left (1 Kings 22:19).

Many people believe the apostle Paul even visited Heaven once before he died. But God would not allow him to tell anybody what he had seen or heard.

The apostle John, who had been such a good friend of Jesus on Earth, saw into Heaven. He wrote about it in the last book of the Bible, called "Revelation." One time he saw a door that suddenly opened right into Heaven! A voice called to him, "Come up here." And before he knew it, he was whisked right through that door and stood before God's mighty throne.

The Bible also tells us about two people who actually went to Heaven to live without dying. One man named Enoch used to take long walks with God every day. (What do you suppose they talked about?) One day he just disappeared from Earth and was taken right into Heaven. The Bible says:

It was by faith that Enoch was taken to Heaven. He never died. He could not be found, because God had taken him away. Before he was taken, the Scripture says that he was a man who truly pleased God (Hebrews 11:5).

I am the light of the world. The person who follows me will never live in darkness. He will have the light that gives life.

JOHN 8:12

25

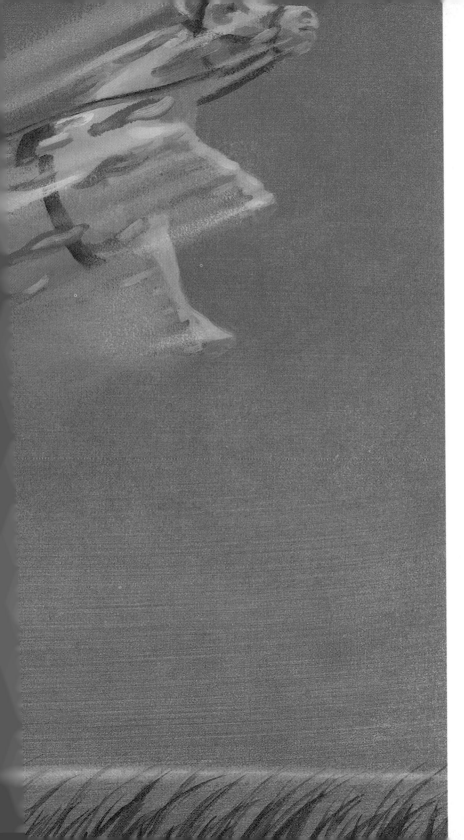

We don't know for sure, but maybe God enjoyed Enoch so much that one day God said to him, "We've walked a long way today, Enoch. It's getting late, and it would be a long walk home for you. Why don't you just come on home with Me?"

So Enoch went home with God. And he didn't even need his sleeping bag or toothbrush!

Elijah was the only man to get to ride to Heaven in a chariot. He was walking along beside his friend Elisha when suddenly a chariot and horses of fire appeared in the middle of a whirl-wind! The chariot took Elijah away. All that was left behind was Elijah's coat. I guess he wasn't going to need it in Heaven. His friend Elisha would need it more.

Everybody else who has gone to Heaven has had to pass through a doorway we call "death." Most people slip through that doorway without telling others what they see. But sometimes people get a peek through the doorway and are able to tell about the shining, happy things on the other side.

One person who looked through that doorway was a young man named Stephen. People who hated the Lord Jesus were throwing rocks at Stephen because he was always talking about his Lord and Friend. The only way they could make him be quiet was to kill him.

Just as he was about to die, he saw the door of Heaven open to let him in. And what he saw through that door made him glad, even though he was hurting so much.

He looked up to Heaven and saw the glory of God. He saw Jesus standing at God's right side. He said, "Look! I see Heaven open. And I see the Son of Man standing at God's right side!" (Acts 7:55-56).

I saw the Lord sitting on his throne. His Heavenly army was standing near him on his right and on his left.

1 KINGS 22:19

27

When Jesus comes back to Earth, all who love Him and belong to Him will never die. The Bible says that our bodies will be changed in a blink and we'll rush right up into the clouds. The Lord Jesus, the Mighty King of all Kings, will be standing in midair, ready to take us to our new home in Heaven.

Whichever way we go to Heaven will work just fine. We might walk into Heaven through death's doorway. Or we might fly straight up into the sky when Jesus comes back to Earth again. It doesn't matter.

Either way, Jesus is the One who will lead us Home.

WILL ANYONE MEET ME WHEN I GET TO HEAVEN?

When you go over to your best friend's house, isn't it a nice feeling to see him sitting on his front porch, waiting for you? When you get home from school, doesn't it makes you feel good to be met at the door by your mother (especially if she's baked some cookies)?

When you go to your grandparents' house, isn't it fun to see them watching for you through the big front window?

When you go outside to play, doesn't it make you happy to see your dog come running up? It makes you glad that he's so glad to see you, and it's funny to watch him wiggle all over and whack his tail on the ground.

When you get back from a week of camp, doesn't it make you glad to see your parents standing there…waiting and waiting for you to come home?

When people love you, they wait for you. When people love you, they think about you and watch for you and can't wait to see you. Why should it be any different when you walk up the sidewalk to Heaven's front door?

Maybe the people who will smile the biggest welcome will be the ones who prayed for you and taught you about Jesus. How happy they will be to see that you gave your life to the Lord!

Who else will be happy? There surely will be a happy bunch of angels waiting for you to come in the door. The Bible says that whenever anyone believes in Jesus, the angels shout for joy. (Maybe they give each other "high fives," too.)

If someone you love is already in Heaven, I imagine he or she will be watching for you out of the corner of an eye. Somehow, in some way, that person will be listening for your footsteps on Heaven's front porch. And when you walk smiling through that doorway, how happy your loved one will be. Everyone will already be very happy, before you come in the door. But in Heaven, there's no limit to how happy you can be. You can keep piling up good, happy things and never stop.

Who will be the happiest? I'll bet you know.

He's the One who loves you most of all. He's the One who died on the cross for you so that you could be in His house for always and forever.

That's right, Jesus will be happiest of all. Don't you think He might be the first one to hug you when you step into Heaven? And I think I know what He will say:

"Come in! Come in! I've been waiting for you!"

WILL I BE ABLE TO FLY IN HEAVEN?

It will sure be great if we can! How else will we keep up with our new angel friends? The Bible doesn't say whether or not we will actually be able to fly. But it does say that we will have new bodies—bodies like the one the Lord Jesus had after He came out of the grave.

And He did some amazing things with His new body!

He could still eat and drink. His hands and flesh still felt warm and good and solid. And He looked at least something like He had always looked. Some of His friends didn't quite recognize Him at first—but after a while they did.

One time when His friends were in a room with all the doors shut tight and locked, Jesus was suddenly standing right in the middle of them! He could just appear wherever He wanted to be!

Will we be able to do that? Will we be able to travel wherever we want in God's new universe with just a blink of our eyes? We don't know what marvelous things we will be able to do. The Bible says we can't even begin to *imagine* what it will be like.

No one has ever seen this. No one has ever heard about it. No one has ever imagined what God has prepared for those who love him (1 Corinthians 2:9).

Flying sounds like such great fun. It's hard to think of something that might be more fun than soaring up into miles of clear, sunny sky. It would be like diving into the deep end of the world's biggest swimming pool—only you'd be going up instead of down—and you wouldn't have to hold your breath!

What could be more fun than burrowing through a cloud or chasing a rainbow or just floating lazily through the air on your stomach and watching the birds play tag below you?

What could be more fun than that?

We'll just have to wait and find out, won't we?

WILL I NEED MONEY IN HEAVEN?

You will have all that you need in your Forever Home. And you can begin right now putting lots and lots of treasure into the Bank of Heaven. Jesus talked about heavenly treasure and said we ought to store it up. He also said it was a lot better to have riches in Heaven than a bunch of money and stuff piled up here on Earth. Do you remember what He said?

Don't store treasures for yourselves here on earth. Moths and rust will destroy treasures here on earth. And thieves can break into your house and steal the things you have. So store your treasures in heaven. The treasures in heaven cannot be destroyed by moths or rust. And thieves cannot break in and steal that treasure. Your heart will be where your treasure is (Matthew 6:19-21).

What does treasure in Heaven look like?

Is it green paper money? I don't think so. Why would we need it? We won't have to pay for anything in our Father's House. Jesus paid it all.

No one has ever seen this. No one has ever heard about it. No one has ever imagined what God has prepared for those who love him.

1 CORINTHIANS 2:9

31

Will Heaven's money be in gold coins? I don't think so. What good would they be? Even the streets will be paved with gold. Gold will be like the gravel along the roads and the sand on a thousand long beaches. I don't think gold will be very important in Heaven.

Will Heaven's money be beautiful jewels? Probably not. The heavenly city will be full of more sparkling, flashing jewels than you could ever count. Jewels will be like the boards or bricks used to build your house. I don't think they would be much good for money. (Have you ever tried to spend a brick?)

Heaven's riches won't be stacks of paper money. It won't be gold. It won't be jewels. What will this treasure be?

Listen to what Paul said about putting treasure in the Bank of Heaven:

Tell the rich people to do good and to be rich in doing good deeds. Tell them to be happy to give and ready to share. By doing that, they will be saving a treasure for themselves in heaven. That treasure will be a strong foundation. Their future life can be built on that treasure (1 Timothy 6:17-19).

Somehow...don't ask me how...
       the kind,
          good,
             generous,
                loving

things we do for other people here on Earth will save up shining, everlasting treasure for us in our Forever Home.

And somehow...please don't ask me how...

Now we hope for the blessings God has for his children. These blessings are kept for you in heaven. They cannot be destroyed or be spoiled or lose their beauty.

1 PETER 1:3-4

33

it will be the kind of treasure that we will want very much,

it will be the kind of treasure that will make us and others very happy,

it will be the kind of treasure that will bring us more and more AND MORE joy in that joyful place.

Will this treasure gleam like white snow in the morning sun?

Will it shimmer like a gold and purple sunset on a still lake?

Will it help us to see our Heavenly Father in some new way? Will it open up new worlds for us to see and rule and build? Will it prepare us for some special heavenly job or an exciting heavenly adventure?

God doesn't tell us that part. But He DOES say we can begin saving now. And He DOES say we'll be glad we did! Have you put any treasure in the Bank of Heaven today?

Now we hope for the blessings God has for his children. These blessings are kept for you in heaven. They cannot be destroyed or be spoiled or lose their beauty (1 Peter 1:4).

Crying may last for a night. But joy comes in the morning.
PSALM 30:5

34

WILL I EVER BE SAD IN HEAVEN?

The Bible says that when we first get to Heaven, God will wipe away all the tears from our eyes. And then it says: *There will be no more death, sadness, crying, or pain. All the old ways are gone (Revelation 21:4).*

Will there be a little sadness left when we first step into Heaven? Could there be a few hurts that haven't been soothed away? Might there be a few tears that just started from our eyes when we left the Earth? If we have just slipped through the doorway called "death," we may feel sad for the pain we felt or the people we had to leave behind.

Who will comfort us? God Himself! He will softly wipe the tears from our eyes. He may whisper, "Don't cry. You're Home now! Everything will be all right now. I am with you always—and now you will always be with Me."

By the time He has wiped away our tears and held us close for a while, the sadness will all be gone. And it will never come again.

In one of his many songs, King David wrote, *Crying may last for a night. But joy comes in the morning (Psalm 30:5).* Heaven will be like one beautiful, joyful morning that goes on and on forever.

Heaven will be so full of God there won't be any room for sad thoughts or old hurts or unhappy memories. God's love will fill up the air like bright sunbeams that fill a summer morning. God's kindness and joy will ripple across the heavenly land like a breeze that touches every flower.

Sadness and tears will be left so far behind they will never catch up to us again.

WHY DOES MY GREAT-GRANDMA WANT TO GO TO HEAVEN EVEN MORE THAN STAYING HERE WITH US?

When people have loved the Lord Jesus for many, many years, something surprising begins to happen. The older they get, and the longer they walk with Jesus, the more they love life on the Heaven side of the door instead of the Earth side. A grandma or great-grandma who loves Jesus very much might say,

"My mamma and daddy have been in Heaven a long time. It's been so long since I've seen them. My brother went to Heaven when he was just a baby. He was so cute! My two sisters went to Heaven when they were grown-up ladies. My own daughter went to Heaven when she was just a little girl with pigtails, and oh—how I miss her.

"Most of my friends have left to be with Jesus. And my wonderful husband went on through Heaven's door just last year. I miss my family and my friends. I can't wait to be with them. I have friends here, but MORE friends over there. I'm ready to go, too, when Jesus calls for me. Seeing Him will be the best of all!"

Even the apostle Paul, who had many, many friends and much important work to do, couldn't seem to make up his mind where he wanted to be:

To me the only important thing about living is Christ. And even death would be profit for me. If I continue living in the body, I will be able to work for the Lord. But what should I choose—living or dying? I do not know. It is hard to choose between the two. I want to leave this life and be with Christ. That is much better. But you need me here in my body...so I know that I will stay with you (Philippians 1:21-25).

Once we have trusted the Lord Jesus as Savior, He will be with us whichever side of the door we are on!

35

WILL THERE BE OTHER CHILDREN IN HEAVEN?

Will there be children in Heaven? Children laughing on golden playgrounds? Children playing tricks on angels? Children running and skipping and turning cartwheels around the feet of Jesus as He walks Heaven's rolling meadows and skips rocks in Heaven's deep lakes?

The Bible doesn't tell us as much as we might like to know. But Jesus did say some very important things about children and Heaven.

One day some parents were bringing their girls and boys to Jesus so that He could put His hands on them and pray for them. The Lord's followers tried to stop them. They probably said, "Don't bother the Lord with all those children! He's too busy. He's too important. He doesn't have time for a bunch of noisy, squirmy, squirrely kids. Go away!"

What do you suppose Jesus thought about that? The Bible says He was displeased. And then He said something that surprised His followers very much:

"Let the little children come to me. Don't stop them. The kingdom of God belongs to people who are like these little children. I tell you the truth. You must accept the kingdom of God as a little child accepts things, or you will never enter it." Then Jesus took the children in his arms. He put his hands on them and blessed them (Mark 10:14-16).

Another time these same men were asking who would be the most important in Heaven. To answer their question, Jesus did

You must accept the kingdom of God as a little child accepts things, or you will never enter it.

MARK 10:15

37

another surprising thing. He called a little child over to Him. (And I'm sure that child ran like a flash to be with Jesus!) Then Jesus had the child stand there in front of all His men. That little one must have looked around with wide eyes at all those serious, bearded faces, and then back at Jesus. Do you suppose Jesus winked at her?

Then he said, *I tell you the truth. You must change and become like little children. If you don't do this, you will never enter the kingdom of Heaven. The greatest person in the kingdom of Heaven is the one who makes himself humble like this child (Matthew 18:3-4).*

Children all over the world love Jesus, and Jesus loves them! And Jesus tells grown-up men and women that they have to become like children even to get into Heaven. Instead of being proud or hard-hearted or stubborn, they need to run gladly into our Lord's wide open arms like little boys and girls. They need to trust Jesus with all their hearts and let Him take care of them.

Children who trust Jesus as their Lord and Savior will be in Heaven. And whether they will be little or big once they get there isn't important. The important thing is that they will be with Jesus forever and ever.

And grownups who trust Jesus in the same way will get to come, too!

WILL I BE AN ANGEL WHEN I GET TO HEAVEN?

No, you won't be an angel. You will be yourself! People and angels are both creations of God, but they are very different. And they will be different in Heaven, too. God created lots and lots of angels way back in the beginning. God has enjoyed them very much, and they have enjoyed Him and served Him with glad hearts.

But even after He had created the beautiful angels who sang and praised Him and shone in the heavens like stars bursting for joy—even after that God had something more in His heart. He wanted to create again. He wanted to create a man and a woman out of the dust of the ground.

How the angels—wide-eyed with delight—must have watched Him as He scooped the dirt into His hands and gently formed the first people who ever were. He loved these people very much, just as He loved the angels.

But something happened to those precious people. They disobeyed God and got into horrible trouble. Things were so bad that no one would have ever been able to go to Heaven if God hadn't done something to help. He loved us so much He sent His own Son, the Lord Jesus, to rescue people like you and me.

What a thing to happen! The Bible says that angels are so curious and so amazed about all of this! They wonder and wonder about what God did to save these men and women and boys and girls.

So when you get to Heaven, you will probably meet angels

who will get excited and nudge one another and say, "Look! There is one of those special people that the Lord Jesus saved for Himself!"

And maybe you will get the chance to sit down with one or two of them in a field of flowers beside a golden road and tell all about it.

WILL EVERYONE GO TO HEAVEN?

The Bible says that God wants everyone to come live in His Forever Home. But the very hard, very sad truth is that there are many, many people who choose not to go to Heaven. Those who choose not to receive God's gift of eternal life in the Lord Jesus will not be in Heaven after they die.

It is the hardest, most heartbreaking truth we can ever think about. But hard as it may be, it is a very important thing to remember. People who turn away from God's wonderful gift will have to go away from Him forever. When they go through death's door, they will find Heaven's door closed and locked. They will be left outside. They will be away from Heaven's brightness and joy and beauty. They will be away from the love and kindness and comfort of the Heavenly Father. And they will never, never be able to change their minds or come back.

That's why it's so important to tell people about the Lord Jesus dying on the cross for our sins. He loves to forgive people and open His arms to people and take lots and lots of people to His Father's House.

All people have sinned and are not good enough for God's glory.

ROMANS 3:23

We must remember how kind our God is. Even when people call out to Jesus to forgive them at the very last minute before they die, He will still take them to Heaven. (Remember what happened to the man on the cross next to Jesus!) And you and I can never REALLY know what people pray in their hearts in those last minutes and seconds before they die. We may be surprised to see who will be in Heaven! But we should never be surprised at how much God loves people and wants to bring them to His beautiful home.

HOW CAN I KNOW FOR SURE I'M GOING TO HEAVEN?

Going to Heaven is so important, you want to be very, very sure that's where you'll be when the time comes to leave this life. And you *can* be sure. You don't have to wonder. You don't have to be afraid or worry.

Jesus came all the way from Heaven to make the way plain and clear. He said:

I tell you the truth. Whoever hears what I say and believes in the One who sent me has eternal life. He will not be judged guilty. He has already left death and has entered into life (John 5:24).

Paul wanted to make the way plain and clear, too. He wrote:

All people have sinned and are not good enough for God's glory....When someone sins, he earns what sin pays—death. But God gives us a free gift—life forever in Christ Jesus our Lord (Romans 3:23; 6:23).

John wanted us to understand, too. He wrote these words about Jesus:

To all who received him, to those who believed in his name, he gave the right to become children of God (John 1:12, NIV).

When you are ready to give your life to Jesus, you might say a prayer to Him something like this.

Dear Lord Jesus,
thank You for inviting me
to Your beautiful Forever Home.
Thank You for inviting me to be a child of God.
Thank You for bleeding and dying on the cross
for all the bad, hurtful things
I have done.
I want to belong to You.
I want You to be Lord and King of my life.
Please forgive me
for the bad things in my heart.
I want my life to belong to You right now
and forever!
Please come into my life and be with me always.
Amen.

Did you pray that prayer? Did you understand it? Did you mean it with all your heart?

Then watch for me when you come to Heaven someday! And I'll be watching for you, too!

*To all
who received him,
to those who
believed in his
name, he gave the
right to become
children of God.*
JOHN 1:12

43

A NOTE FROM THE AUTHOR...

I hope you enjoy as much as I do artist Tim Jonke's sensitive, dream-like illustrations in this little book. Just as we must do, Tim has imagined a great many things about our eternal state, since God has revealed comparatively little about it.

Some readers may disagree with certain aspects of how heaven or its inhabitants are portrayed here. In particular, some Christians today have objected to the depiction of heavenly beings with wings. This, however, seems to me an issue on which the Bible is quite specific. For example, the Lord was precise in His instructions on how to portray cherubim in the furnishings of the tabernacle and temple. If these mighty angels have wings, who is to say other angelic beings would not? (See Exodus 25:20 and 37:9; 1 Kings 6:24-27 and 8:6-7; 1 Chronicles 28:18; 2 Chronicles 3:11-13 and 5:7-8; Isaiah 6:2; Ezekiel 1:6-11, 1:24-25, 3:13, 10:5-21, and 11:22; Daniel 9:21; and Revelation 4:8.)

The purpose of *Someday Heaven*, however, isn't to detail angelic anatomies or describe heavenly architecture and landscaping. This book's purpose is to help us set our hearts on our promised future home and inheritance, and—most of all—to increase our longing for the One who died and rose again to bring us there. Praise His Name!